ANIMAL EXTREMES

SMALLEST SPECIES

BY ELISABETH NORTON

WWW.APEXEDITIONS.COM

Apex is distributed by North Star Editions:
sales@northstareditions.com | 888-417-0195

Produced for Apex by Red Line Editorial.

Photographs ©: Shutterstock Images, cover, 4–5, 8, 14, 18–19, 21, 22–23; Frank Glaw, Jörn Köhler, Ted M. Townsend, Miguel Vences/Public Library of Science, 1, 7; Frank Glaw, Jörn Köhler, Oliver Hawlitschek, Fanomezana M. Ratsoavina, Andolalao Rakotoarison, Mark D. Scherz, & Miguel Vences, 6, 29; Chris Austin/CB2/ZOB/LSU supplied by WENN.com/Newscom, 10–11; iStockphoto, 12–13; Mariano Sayno/Moment/Getty Images, 15; Dr. Harold Rose/Science Source, 16–17; Ben Sale/Flickr, 20; Peter Morris/The Sydney Morning Herald/Fairfax Media/ Getty Images, 24; Yevgen Kiosya, Katarzyna Vončina, Piotr Gąsiorek/Evolutionary Systematics, 25; Matt Wilson and Jay Clark/NOAA, 26; NOAA OKEANOS EXPLORER Program, Oceano Profundo 2015/NOAA, 27

Library of Congress Control Number: 2022919898

ISBN
978-1-63738-532-6 (hardcover)
978-1-63738-586-9 (paperback)
978-1-63738-693-4 (ebook pdf)
978-1-63738-640-8 (hosted ebook)

Printed in the United States of America
Mankato, MN
082023

NOTE TO PARENTS AND EDUCATORS

Apex books are designed to build literacy skills in striving readers. Exciting, high-interest content attracts and holds readers' attention. The text is carefully leveled to allow students to achieve success quickly. Additional features, such as bolded glossary words for difficult terms, help build comprehension.

TABLE OF CONTENTS

CHAPTER 1

LITTLE LIZARDS

A team of scientists walk through a forest. They are searching for chameleons. Several types of these lizards live only in Madagascar. Some are very small.

More than 100 different types of chameleons live in Madagascar.

On this trip, the scientists find a new kind of chameleon. It is the smallest **reptile** in the world. It's about the size of a sunflower seed.

The smallest chameleon is 0.85 inches (21.6 mm) long from head to tail.

Before 2021, *Brookesia micra* was the smallest known type of chameleon.

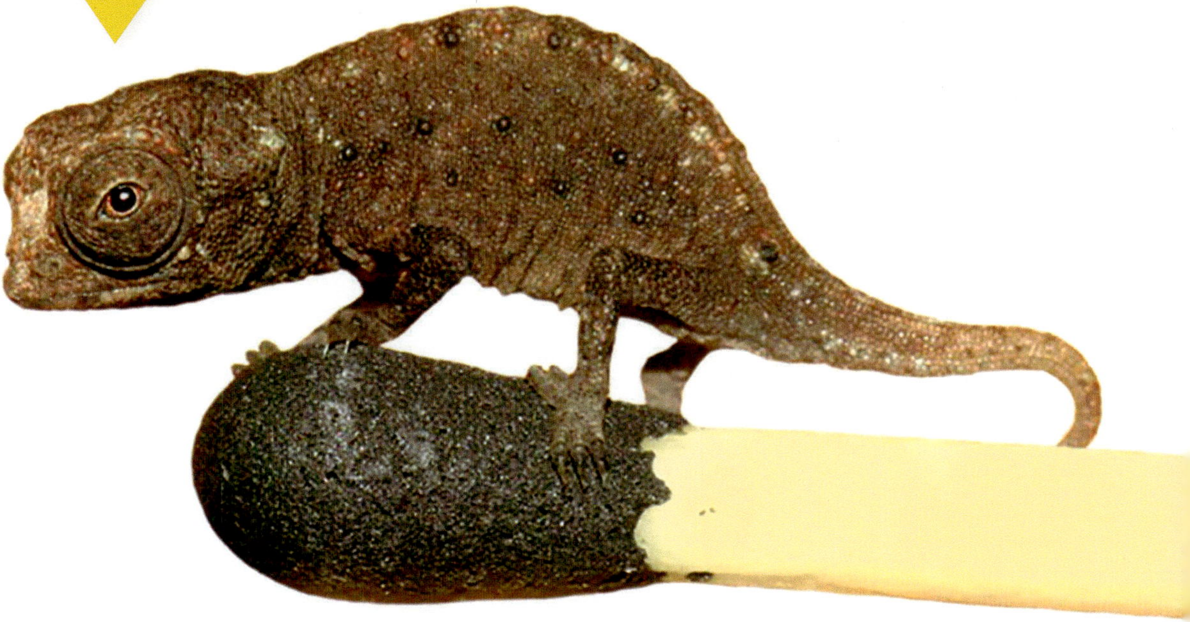

FAST FACT

The new chameleon **species** is called *Brookesia nana*. It was found in 2021.

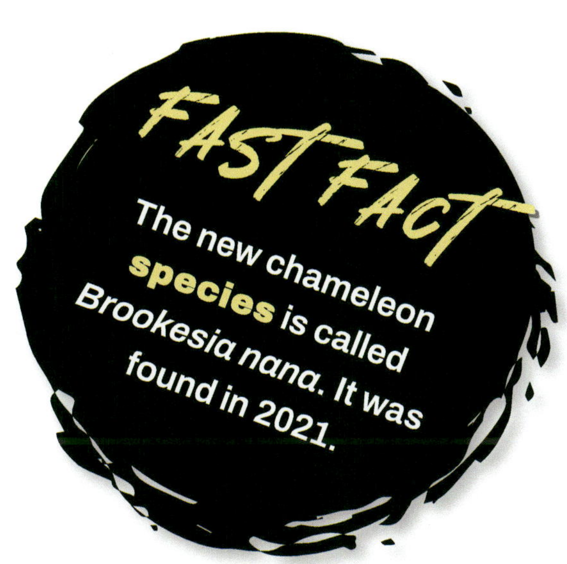

The scientists find two of these chameleons. One is male. The other is female. The scientists are excited to learn more about them.

MADAGASCAR

Madagascar is an island off Africa's eastern coast. It is home to many unique species. It has plants and animals that don't live anywhere else on Earth.

Tiny chameleons often hide in leaves on the forest floor.

CHAPTER 2

VERTEBRATES

A frog species is the smallest **vertebrate**. The frog lives in jungles in New Guinea. It is 0.3 inches (7.7 mm) long. That's about the size of a housefly.

The world's tiniest frog is smaller than a dime.

The smallest bird is the bee hummingbird. It is just 2.25 inches (5.7 cm) long.

FAST FACT

Bee hummingbird nests are the size of a quarter. The bird's eggs are the size of peas.

The bumblebee bat has a wingspan of about 5 inches (12.7 cm).

The bumblebee bat is the smallest **mammal**. Its body measures just over 1 inch (2.5 cm) long. And it weighs about as much as a dime.

SMALLEST SNAKE

The Barbados threadsnake grows just 4.1 inches (10.4 cm) long. It is as thin as a spaghetti noodle. And it can curl up on a quarter.

The tiny Barbados threadsnake digs burrows in the ground.

CHAPTER 3

INSECTS

Fairyflies are the smallest insects in the world. Some are just 127 **micrometers** long. That is about the width of a hair.

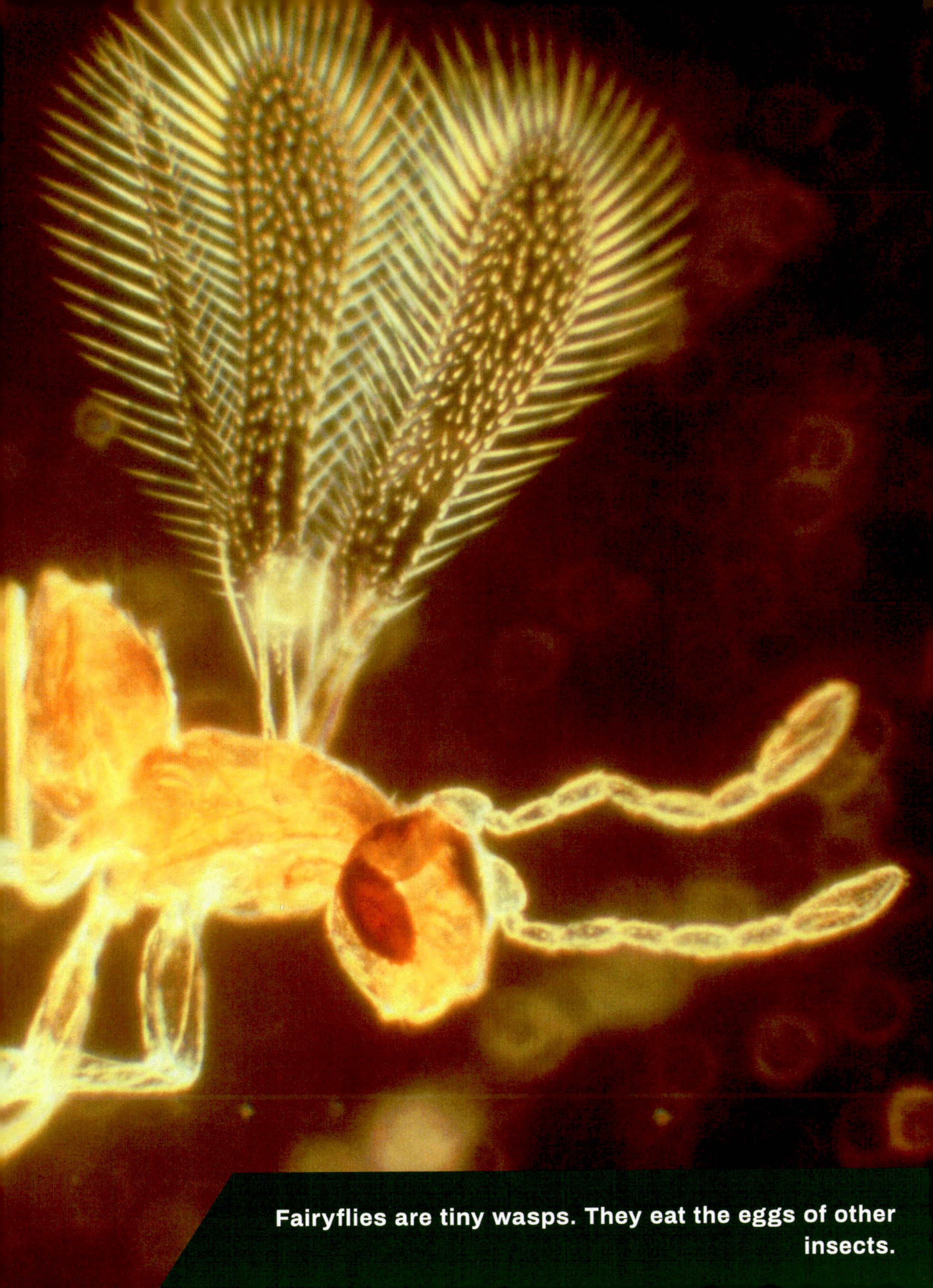

Fairyflies are tiny wasps. They eat the eggs of other insects.

Scarlet dwarf dragonflies live in Asia.

The smallest flies are 395 micrometers long. They are parasites. They live in ant nests and eat the ants.

The pygmy sorrel moth is the world's smallest moth. Its wingspan is just 0.104 inches (2.65 mm). A grain of rice is about that thick.

Pygmy sorrel moths are part of a group of small moths called leaf miners.

Leaf miner caterpillars eat tunnels through leaves.

TINY SPIDERS

Spiders aren't insects. They are **arachnids**. The smallest spider is the *Patu digua*. Males grow just 370 micrometers. That's smaller than the head of a pin.

CHAPTER 4

WATER CREATURES

Many small species live in water. One is the pygmy seahorse. It can be less than 1 inch (2.5 cm) long.

Pygmy seahorses often live near corals or water plants.

The smallest fish can be less than 0.32 inches (8 mm) long. One is the Stout infantfish. Its length is less than the width of a pencil.

Of the three smallest species of fish, the Stout infantfish is the lightest.

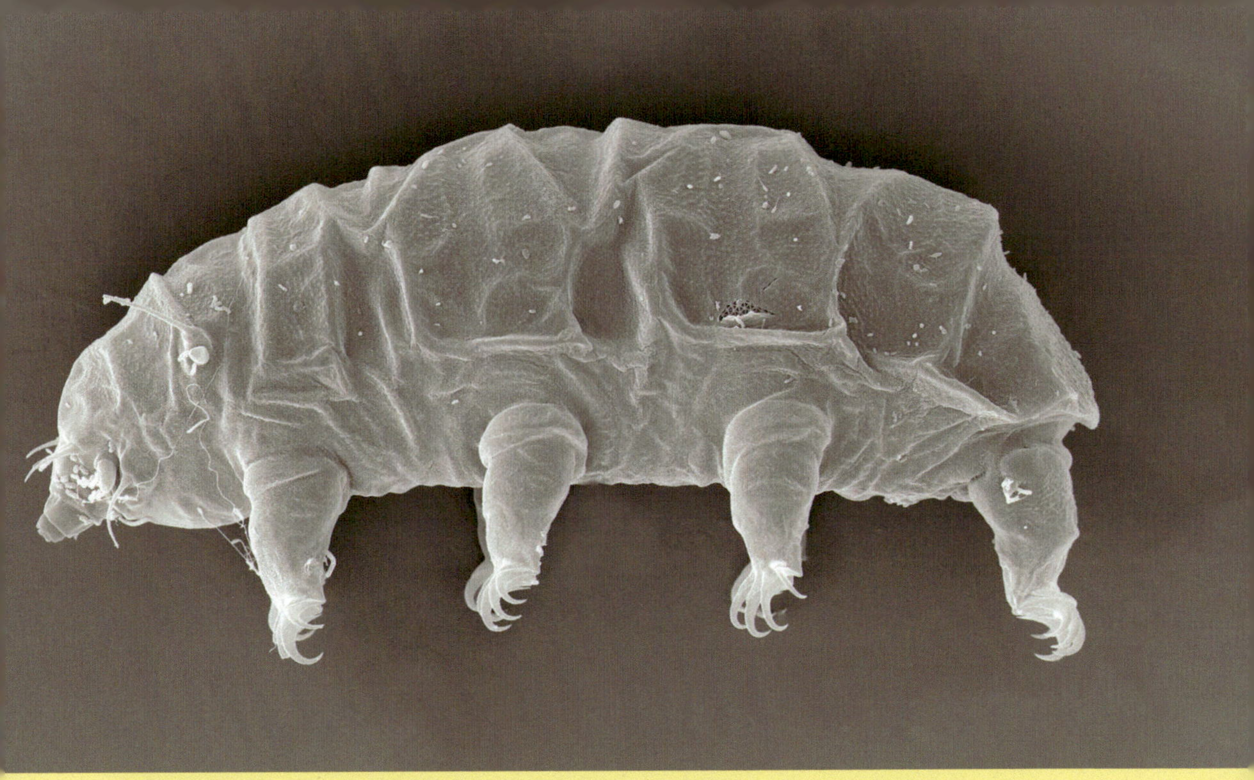

Tardigrades often live in or near water. But they can survive extreme heat, cold, or dryness.

FAST FACT

Tardigrades are tiny animals with eight legs. Most grow just 0.02 inches (0.5 mm) long.

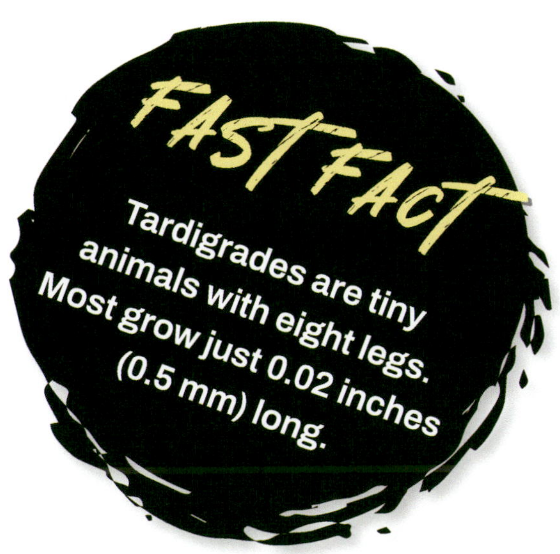

Zooplankton drift through the water.

The smallest animals in the ocean are zooplankton. Some can only be seen with a **microscope**. They are a key source of food for other ocean animals.

CORALS

Coral reefs are made up of tiny animals called polyps. The polyps look like tubes. They have mouths and **tentacles**. Many polyps join together to form reefs.

Coral polyps stick their tentacles out into the water to catch food, such as zooplankton.

COMPREHENSION QUESTIONS

Write your answers on a separate piece of paper.

1. Write a sentence describing the main idea of Chapter 1.

2. Would you rather study reptiles, mammals, or insects? Why?

3. What is the smallest insect in the world?

    A. fairyfly
    B. *Patu digua*
    C. pygmy sorrel moth

4. Which of these vertebrates is the smallest?

    A. bee hummingbird
    B. bumblebee bat
    C. Barbados threadsnake

5. What does **unique** mean in this book?

*It is home to many **unique** species. It has plants and animals that don't live anywhere else on Earth.*

A. living in many places
B. exactly like all others
C. different from all others

6. What does **parasites** mean in this book?

*They are **parasites**. They live in ant nests and eat the ants.*

A. animals that are too small to see
B. animals that eat fruits and seeds
C. animals that live on or in other animals

Answer key on page 32.

GLOSSARY

arachnids

Animals with hard outer bodies and eight legs, such as scorpions and spiders.

mammal

An animal that has hair and produces milk for its young.

micrometers

Very small units of measurement. One micrometer equals 0.000039 inch (0.001 mm).

microscope

A tool that makes very small things look bigger.

reptile

A cold-blooded animal that has scales.

species

A group of animals or plants that are similar and can breed with one another.

tentacles

The flexible limbs of animals such as squid or jellyfish.

vertebrate

An animal that has a backbone.

TO LEARN MORE

BOOKS

Kenney, Karen Latchana. *Coral Reefs*. Minneapolis: Bellwether Media, 2022.

London, Martha. *Hummingbirds*. Minneapolis: Abdo Publishing, 2020.

Orr, Tamra B. *Animal Discoveries*. North Mankato, MN: Capstone Press, 2019.

ONLINE RESOURCES

Visit **www.apexeditions.com** to find links and resources related to this title.

ABOUT THE AUTHOR

Elisabeth Norton is originally from the United States. Now she lives with her family in Switzerland, where she is an English teacher and writer.

INDEX

ANSWER KEY:
1. Answers will vary; 2. Answers will vary; 3. A; 4. B; 5. C; 6. C